KATHARIN OUR NOR' QUEEN

The Life And Northern Associations Of
Queen Katharine Parr, The Last Wife
Of King Henry VIII.

COMPILED & WRITTEN
BY
KEITH SNOWDEN

CASTLEDEN PUBLICATIONS
PICKERING

ISBN 0-9514657-7-5

First published 1994
Reprinted 1997
Reprinted 2001

Typeset, Printed & Bound
at the press of the publisher:
CASTLEDEN PUBLICATIONS.
11 Castlegate, Pickering, North
Yorkshire, YO18 7AX.
Tel: 01751-476227.

INTRODUCTION

SOME YEARS ago I started to write a novel covering the life and marriages of Queen Katharine Parr, the last queen of King Henry VIII. The novel was about half-written when I took to writing local and regional history books. In the course of my studies for the novel I visited many places where Katharine Parr had lived. I prayed in chapels and churches where she had worshipped and I paced in rooms where she had walked. I looked into the chamber where her daughter was born, and where Katharine probably died.

This book is about her life and her associations with the North of England. There is no space here for the bungled diplomacy of King Henry and his many intrigues, except where it touches Katharine and those close to her, for we are concentrating on the human relationships.

I have tried to make it as accurate as possible, drawing heavily on Agnes Strickland's *Lives of the Queens of England*, contrasting her account from many other sources.

The photographs were taken by myself while on my tours of research.

K.S.
Pickering,
1994.

ACKNOWLEDGEMENTS

TO THE Head Librarian at the Kendal Library, for allowing me to spend many hours in the Local History Section, during which I studied, amongst other matter, unpublished manuscripts as follows:

Chapters In The History Of Kendal, by R.H.Pilling.

The Parrs Of Kendal, by Susan Elizabeth James.

CHILDHOOD

KATHARINE PARR was born at Kendal Castle, West-morland, about 1513. Some authorities give the date as 1512, but it will become evident, from the mention later of certain documents, that 1513 is the more likely date. She was the first daughter of Sir Thomas Parr, who held land at Horton, Northamptonshire, and who had a quarter share in the barony of Kendal. Sir Thomas was a courtier, friend and boon companion of King Henry VIII; one of a group of young men who travelled around with 'Bluff King Hal' on his frequent fun-seeking jaunts, many of which were on the River Thames in his great royal barge.

Sir Thomas's mother was Elizabeth, the daughter of Henry, Lord Fitz-Hugh and Alice, the daughter of Richard Neville, Earl of Salisbury. Her first husband was Sir William Parr. Thomas Parr married Matilda, (otherwise Maude), a younger daughter of Sir Thomas Greenes of Boughton and Greens Norton, Northamptonshire. Sir Thomas could claim in his ancestry links with some of the greatest baronial families in the North of England, including Marmion, de Roos, de Lancaster, and Neville.

Sir Thomas Parr had been at Court since 1500 and he was elevated to Controller of the King's Household. As Sir Thomas rose in power the family influence was moved away from Kendal to Northamptonshire, and the Parr's lands at Kendal were administered by the Stricklands of Sizergh. There had been a link between the Stricklands and Parrs since the 14th century, when the granddaughter of Sir Thomas Strickland married Sir William de Parre. The link was renewed in 1464, when another Sir Thomas wed Agnes Parre. A further connection came when in 1515 Sir Walter Strickland married Katherine Neville, the co-heiress of Thornton Bridge, Brafferton, Yorkshire. It was in that same year that Katharine Parr's sister, Anne, was born.

1

So much did the king trust Sir Thomas Parr that he chose him along with his brother William Parr to go to York on April 14th,1516, to meet Henry's sister, Margaret Tudor, Queen of Scotland. At her father's wish Margaret had married James IV of Scotland in an effort to settle affairs between the two countries. Unfortunately, matters were not so easily mended and the Scottish king had been killed in the Battle of Flodden Field, three years earlier.

At this time the Parr's were blessed with the birth of a son, named William after his grandfather. They had a house in Blackfriars where they lived when at Court. Lady Parr had become a Lady-in-waiting to Queen Catherine of Aragon, Henry's first wife and widow of his elder brother, Arthur, Prince of Wales, who had died of consumption at the age of fifteen. Henry had only been fifteen himself when his father had forced him to marry Catherine.

Just as Sir Thomas Parr's star seemed to be so promisingly in the ascendancy, he suddenly died in 1517, and was buried in Blackfriars Church. In his will he left his two daughters £800 between them as marriage dowries. He stipulated that Katharine should marry a peer or the son of a peer. For all Lady Parr was only twentytwo when she became a widow, she resisted any urge she may have felt to marry again. She was allowed to keep her position as Lady-in-waiting to the queen, and she concentrated her efforts on training her daughters for the high life of society. Katharine was gifted by nature with fine qualities and talents. She both wrote and read Latin with ease, had some knowledge of Greek, and was well versed in modern languages. It would appear that Katharine was capable of producing needlework of a high quality and there are examples of her handiwork in the form of a tablecloth and a counterpane of white satin embroidered with pictures of flowers, gorgeous birds and butterflies, said to have been worked by her, and shown to visitors at Sizergh Castle. The friend and companion of her childhood and early youth was Elizabeth Bellingham, daughter and co-heiress of Sir Robert Bellingham of Burneside, near Kendal.

Lady Parr was anxious to procure a noble husband for the young Katharine, but there was little choice at Court, so she enlisted the aid of her cousin Thomas, Lord Dacre, in 1524, to find a suitable candidate.Lord Dacre had a grandson, the thirteen year old son and heir of Henry, Lord Scrope of Masham. It is to some letters preserved among the Scrope manuscripts that we learn that Katharine was not yet twelve years of age, so she could not have been born before 1513.Lord Dacre was anxious that his young grandson could indulge in the liberal education which Lady Parr's children were enjoying. It was customary to write certain safeguards into a marriage contract between such young partners in case one of them died, or if they 'failed to reach carnal copulation'. The Scropes were a famous Northern family which had given England one queen, one Prince of Wales, a cardinal and three archbishops, as well as many other high ranking churchmen and knights. But the family had had it's share of misfortune, and they were not as wealthy as the Parrs. As Katharine's dowry was so small, the negotiations failed on a financial basis. Lady Parr took advice from Cuthbert Tunstall, the friend of her late husband and at that time Bishop of London. She wrote to Lord Scroope to cancel the contract of marriage.

It was then necessary to begin a new search and this resulted in a man who was related to the Parrs through the Fitz-Hugh side of the family.

THE FIRST MARRIAGE

EDWARD BURGH,2nd Lord Borough of Gainsborough Lincolnshire, was a widower in his early sixties. His first wife was Anne, heiress of Sir Thomas Cobham,

3

through whom Lord Borough had obtained a number of estates in Kent. His mother was Margaret Roos, which would appear to have a link with the Parr's ancestors. After his marriage to Katharine, there was a further link when Lord Borough's second son, Henry, married Katharine Neville, widow of Sir Walter Strickland of Sizergh, who died in 1528. Lord Borough had four grown up sons at the time of his marriage to Katharine; the eldest was Thomas, who married Agnes Tyrwhitt, the others being Henry, George and Humphrey. The first Lord Borough had been a Yorkist in the War of the Roses and he had helped King Edward IV escape from Middleham Castle in Yorkshire where he was held a prisoner. That had been in 1469 and the following year extensive damage had been done to Gainsborough Hall by the Lancastrians, as a reprisal. Lord Thomas had soon set about repairing the damage and he had added some improvements to the building. He had entertained King Richard III there in 1484.

Lord Borough was a member of a family with an ancient name: de Burgh. One of these, Richard de Burgh was known as The Red Earl of Ulster, in the 14th century. This earl was father-in-law of Robert Bruce, king of Scotland, and was arrested when the Scots invaded Ireland in 1315, in case he should render aid to Bruce. During the reign of Edward III, William de Burgh, Earl of Ulster, had his only daughter betrothed to Lionel of Antwerp, the king's son. This earl also represented on the distaff side the great Marcher house of Clare. At Catterick, in North Yorkshire there are brasses of Catherine de Burgh and her son, who built the chancel, nave and aisles of the church in 1415; and brasses of William de Burgh of 1442, and his son, also William, of 1492 and his wife. Serlo de Burgh is said to have built the castle at Knaresborough in the 12th century. In the time of King John, a Hubert de Burgh was made regent in 1219. William Shakespeare

characterised him in *The Life and Death of King John.*
Young as she was, we can be certain that Katharine would have been well grounded in those qualities and graces befitting the lady of a lord, and it would be her duty to administer an household staff of something like one hundred servants at the Old Hall. Katharine and her lord were married, probably in 1527. No children came of this alliance.

It was during these early years that the first rumblings in the Church began to be heard, which would play such a significant part in Katharine's later life. In 1517, Martin Luther nailed his nninetyfive theses to the church door in Wittenburg. A Papal Bull had been issued in 1520 containing his excommunication, which he burned in public. In the following year he defied the emperor Charles V at the Diet of Worms. England had seen an earlier attempt at reformation in the person of John Wycliffe, who was born at Hipswell, near Richmond, Yorkshire, in 1320. Educated at Balliol, he was appalled at the abuses and wealth of the Church. His aim was to clear away the superstitions and its aim for wealth and power. Wycliffe also made a translation of the Bible into English, so that it might be easier understood by the ordinary people.

Katharine's first marriage was short-lived, for Lord Borough died in 1528. The young widow was now the dowager Lady Borough and she was known as a 'King's Widow', which meant that she would be under the protection of the monarch and would not be able to marry again without his permission. Katharine was fifteen now and a woman of some means, although the vast bulk of her husband's estate went to his sons, Katharine did receive some property.

According to Agnes Strickland in her *Lives of the Queens of England,* soon after the death of Lord Borough, Katharine was bereaved of her mother and she considered it wise to take up residence with Lady

Strickland at Sizergh, whom, according to the quaint custom of the time, she called her 'good mother'. Lady Strickland held of the Crown the wardship of her son, young Walter Strickland's person and estates; she remained mistress of Sizergh Castle, even after her marriage to Henry Borough. Yet some records show that Lady Parr died in 1532. Certainly Katharine may have spent some time at Sizergh, for they have a room there called 'The Queen's Room', which she is purported to have occupied during her stay. But, if there was this four year gap between the deaths of Lord Borough and Lady Parr, it seems more likely that Katharine would return to London. Now that she was a woman of means and a titled lady, she would be able to attend Court.

If other accounts are to be believed, she returned to the Royal School under the tutorship of Ludovico Vives, a Spanish-born brilliant Humanist scholar, of whom Katharine was said to be one of his best and keenest pupils. He advised Katharine:

> That it did not become a widow to dress up and paint herself, for she should not be seen to seek a marriage bargain, but on the contrary to refuse any that are offered. She should not only speak such words as shall show her to be chaste and honest, but also as shall impress her hearers with her learning, and ammend their ways by the example of her living. All men like to think that they would be missed by their wives after they were dead and a man who might be thinking of marrying a widow would change his mind if he saw her treat widowhood lightly, since he would suppose that she would do the same when his turn came to die. Therefore you should not think of marriage straight away, but observe a reasonable period of mourning.

Ludovico Vives wrote *Apologia sive Confutatio,* a long and competent book on Catherine of Aragon's behalf. His defence of the queen would later lead to his fleeing the country for fear of his life.

6

Kendal Castle

Sizergh Castle

Agnes Strickland avers that at no other period in her life than the interval between her mother's death and her own second marriage could Katharine have found leisure to embroider the magnificent counterpane and toilette-cover, which are shown at Sizergh Castle as trophies of her industry. ' The material on which both counterpane and toilette-cover are worked is the richest white satin, of a fabric with which the production of no modern loom can vie.' [This was written in 1886] 'The centre of the pattern is a medallion, surrounded by a wreath of natural flowers, wrought in twisted silks and bullion. A spread eagle, in bold relief, gorged with an imperial crown, forms the middle. At each corner is a lively heraldic monster of the dragon class, glowing with purple, crimson and gold. The toilette is *En Suite,* but of a similar pattern. The lapse of three centuries has scarcely diminished the brilliancy of the colours, or tarnished the bullion; nor is the purity of the satin sullied, though both these queenly relics have been used, on state occasions by the family in whose possession they have remained as precious heirlooms and memorials of their ancestral connections with Queen Katharine Parr.'

THE SECOND MARRIAGE

IT WAS her good family friend Cuthbert Tunstal who suggested a solution to Katharine's problem of finding a new husband. In 1530, Tunstal had been translated to Durham, one of the most powerful positions in the Church, and at that time would be called a Prince Palatine. The transfer came about by a Papal Bull to appoint a successor to the fallen Cardinal Wolsey. Tunstal told Katharine that he had a friend who lived in the North of Yorkshire, was forty years old and twice widowed, with two young children, a boy and a girl. He was John Neville,Lord Latimer of Danby,to which title he had succeeded in 1530,taking his seat in the House of Lords

the following January. He had served in the French
wars and was the third holder of the new Latimer Foundation. Neville was a distant cousin to Katharine
through his father, Richard Neville, who led the men of
Mashamshire to Victory at Flodden Field,and he became Lieutenant General of the North for Henry VIII.
   John Neville first married Dorothea de Vere, the sister
and co-heiress of John de Vere, 14th Earl of Oxford.
The son, also John, was the result of that marriage.
Dorothea died in 1527 and John then married Elizabeth
Musgrove, who was a daughter of a well-known Border
family, one of whom, Giles Musgrove, spurred King
James of Scotland into battle at Flodden. Elizabeth had
died three years later, so Lord Latimer had been a
widower for three years. His second wife had bore him
a daughter, Margaret. Lord Latimer's main residence
was at Snape, near Bedale, and he had estates at Great
Tanfield, adjoining the former Marmion land, held by
the Parrs. He also had estates at Danby, in Cleveland,
which included a castle; manors at Sinnington, and
Thornton-in-Pickering Lythe [now Thornton-le-Dale],
and Great Ayton. In Worcestershire he owned *Wyke
Hall* estate and the manor of Beoley; in Buckinghamshire the estate of Latimer; and a manor in Northamptonshire. He also had an impressive mansion in the
grounds of Charterhouse, London.
   Katharine was now a fully-grown woman of twenty,
and fairly tall in stature. She was slim with auburn
hair, a firm nose and a tiny mouth. Her oval face, almost pointed, was marred a little by the upward slope
of her eyebrows, which gave her a rather severe appearance. Her disposition, however, was open, friendly
and outgoing.
   Katharine must have felt proud to strengthen her ties
with this great Northern family, whose ancestors had
come over with William of Normandy. In 1174,
Geoffrey Neville married Emma de Bulmer,who was the

9

heiress of Sir Bertram de Bulmer, who was a very powerful baron of Saxon origin, during the reigns of Henry I and Stephen. He owned vast estates in Durham and Yorkshire. Sir Bertram was highly regarded by royalty and held the important office of Sheriff of Yorkshire. With the marriage of Emma to Geoffrey, the properties passed into the ownership of the Nevilles. At Raby Castle there is a *Bulmer Tower,* which is said to be one of the oldest parts of the building. Robert Neville married the daughter of Ralph Fitz-Ranulph and their son, Ralph, became the first Baron Neville of Raby. Robert was known as 'The Peacock of the North' and his grandson, John, was granted a license by the Bishop of Durham in 1378, to build a castle at Raby and a charter to establish a weekly market at Staindrop as well as an annual fair. This John was the son of Ralph Neville, the victor of the Battle of Neville's Cross. John was followed by another Ralph who became the first Earl of Westmorland. This Ralph married for his first wife, Margaret, the daughter of Hugh, Earl of Stafford, and for his second, Joan Beaufort, the daughter of John O' Gaunt. Joan had twentyone children, the youngest, Cicely, who was called 'Proud Cis', but was better known as 'The Rose of Raby', married Richard Plantagenet, the Duke of York, and was thus the mother of Kings Edward IV and Richard III, and consequently the great-grandmother of Henry VIII. The first Earl of Westmorland's son was Richard, Earl of Warwick, generally known as 'The Kingmaker'. Lord Latimer was related to Katharine in about the same degree as her first husband, Lord Borough.

Ralph Fitz-Ranulph first built a manor house on the site at Snape in 1250. Snape means 'bog' and the builders had to sink huge wooden poles, some twelve feet long by eight feet in diameter to secure a sound foundation. Sometime between 1400 and 1423, the old manor was demolished and the house as Katharine saw it, when she arrived in 1533, was built. There was a moat in which fish were kept for Fridays. Lord Latimer and Katharine were married in the private chapel. When they entered the house, they were in for a shock; the whole place was in a state of utter disarray. The rushes on the floor were alive with vermin and lice which were living off decaying food particles. When things were put to rights, there was a staff of about seventy to run the hall. The good temper and sound sense of Katharine taught her to perform the difficult duties that devolved upon her, in the role of a stepmother, with such conscientious gentleness, that she ensured the love of all the families with whom she was connected in that capacity.

Another wedding took place that year – that of King Henry and Anne Boleyn. Early in the year it was discovered that mistress Boleyn was pregnant and so a secret marriage took place on January 25th. Their daughter, Elizabeth, was born on September 7th.

Lord Latimer was a quiet and unambitious man and must have enjoyed visiting his estates in Yorkshire, when not having to be in London. He and Katharine would occasionally stay at Danby Castle, which had been built by Baron le Latymer in the early 14th century. It was rather unique in design for that part of England, being part palace and part stronghold. They had a splendid Hall at Sinnington, which stood behind the church. The Sinnington manor had long been in the family. William, Lord Latymer died in 1381, leaving a daughter and heiress, Elizabeth, who became the second wife of John, Lord Neville of Raby. Their son, another John, inherited Sinnington and was summoned to Parliament as Baron Latymer during the reigns of Henry V and Henry VI. He died childless and his estates devolved upon his nephew, George Neville, the son of Ralph Neville, Earl of Westmorland, who was his father's half-brother. George married Elizabeth Beauchamp, daughter of the Earl of Warwick, and he was summoned to Parliament as Baron Latimer from 1432 to 1469.He was succeeded by his grandson,Richard, who was the father of Katharine's new husband, John. Thornton consisted of four manors, the main one being the property of Lord Latimer and he had a fulling mill there.

The period just ended had been a very disturbing one. From King Henry setting aside Queen Catherine, there were signs of a rebellion. There were no newspapers in those days, but opinions were expressed publicly in sermons. One of the most prominent and first to preach against the divorce was Queen Catherine's confessor, John Forrest, a warder of the Convent at Greenwich, taking a stance which would lead to his eventual execution. Then there was the affair of 'The Nun of Kent', a certain Elizabeth Barton, who had some eight years previous won much notoriety with her prophecies, claiming that she saw visions. In 1527 she began to speak out openly against the divorce and foretold that God would punish the Pope if he gave way to the king. She was exploited by a group of clergy led by Dr.Edward Bocking of Christ Church. Elizabeth was arrested in July 1533 and taken to the Tower of London. Doubtless she would be tortured into providing a list of names of those who had been using her. She was hanged at Tyburn in April of the folloing year, along with Dr.Bocking and four others.

In the New Year of 1534, the king sent for Cuthbert Tunstal to go and declare himself. In the previous autumn he had written a letter to the king, begging him to return to the paths of righteousness before it was too late. Henry had replied in a friendly good-natured tone. Whilst Tunstal was in London, some agents arrived at Aukland Palace and thoroughly went through the bishop's private papers. These spies had been sent by

Thomas Cromwell, who had started sifting out the secrets of the clergy. They did not find any incriminating evidence at Aukland. At that same time, Thomas More was imprisoned in the Tower, awaiting his ultimate death. More had, according to his accusers, been implicated with 'The Nun of Kent'.

Lord Latimer was a Roman Catholic and what must have been even more disturbing to his mind was that some of his own kinsmen had become involved in the affair of the Nun. His brothers, Sir William and Sir Geoffrey Neville had been arrested and questioned. No real evidence could be found against them at the time and they were eventually released. Next, the Countess of Salisbury, whose mother was a Neville, fell under suspicion. Her father was the Dule of Clarence, brother of King Edward IV, the 'Sun in Splendour'. Her own brother had been murdered by King Henry's father to secure his tentative hold on the Crown. Margaret Plantagenet had been made Countess of Salisbury to compenate her for the loss of the many honours of her house. Margaret had married Richard Pole, Earl of Suffolk and after his death on the battlefield in 1525, she was treated with full respect by the king and was elected to preside over Princess Mary's household. Richard de la Pole, a nephew of Edward IV, had more than once tried to cause an uprising in England and consequently thought it politic to remain abroad, where he sided with the French against England.Richard was known as 'The White Rose' and considered to be the main upholder of the Plantagenet cause. The Countess of Salisbury had remained aloof from him and had never been suspected of associating with Pole's aspirations and dangerous rebellions.

Margaret's eldest son, Reginald Pole, was at the time of his mother's arrest living abroad, as he was hostile to the king's divorce. As a main descendant of the Plantagenets he was regarded with great importance in the eyes of foreign rulers. Reginald Pole had been well educated at the Carthusion school at Sheen, at Magdalen College, Oxford, and at Padua. King Henry had paid a great deal towards this education. His tutors at Oxford had been Thomas Linacre and Hugh Latimer, both noted reformers. On the death of Wolsey, Pole was urged to accept the bishopric of Winchester, or the archbishopric of York, the king being anxious to win Pole over to his side in the conflict with the Pope. Reginald would not accept Henry's terms and they quarrelled violently. Henry forgave him and allowed him to go abroad again. However, when ordered to return and declare his allegiance, he had refused all such commands. It seems the Nun of Kent had been in touch with him and had made predictions and informed him of her plans. Margaret still had two sons in England, Lord Montague and Geoffrey Pole, as well as her cousin, Henry Courtney, Marquis of Exeter, who was a grandson of Edward IV, and, with the exception of the Duke of Norfolk, was the most powerful nobleman in the realm.

Lord Latimer was summoned to Parliament in November 1534. The first act of the session was to pass the bill which named the king as 'the only supreme Head of the Church of England'. It gave the king full powers to enforce his authority and the right to punish any who stood against him. The old Pope, Clement, had died and Pope Paul III had been elected in his place.

Two of the highest churchmen in the land were executed the following year; John Fisher, Bishop of Rochester, who was born and educated at Beverley, and was at one time vicar of Northallerton, was beheaded on June 22nd; and Thomas More on July 6th.

In February 1536, Anne Boleyn miscarried with a dead boy, which could only add to Henry's displeasure. He had been regarding her with suspicion for some time. For his own part, it is fairly evident that he was

14

flirting with Jane Seymour as early as September,1534. Life was becoming increasingly busy and less peaceful with the problems besetting King Henry, necessitating Lord Latimer's presence at Parliament. On May 12th, 1536, Lord Latimer wrote from Snape to Thomas Cromwell:

It is reported that the Lords shall be sent for to come up shortly. I beg you will have me excused by reason of business in Worcestershire. I have been at every prorogation and session of the last Parliament since it began, which has been very painful and chargeable to me.

Unfortunately this truancy put Lord Latimer in Cromwell's black books, for because of his absence, he missed the trial of Anne Boleyn, and to make matters worse, Cromwell did not receive the letter until after the trial had taken place, for it was held on the very day that Lord Latimer had written his letter. There was an immediate response in that Latimer and Katharine were ordered to be in London by June 8th, when Parliament was to be assembled for the proclamation of Jane Seymour as Anne Boleyn's successor. Poor Anne, she had failed to provide Henry with a son and heir. Reading of her trial today, it seems like a trumped up affair and was carried out with indecent haste. She was beheaded on May 19th, just one week after Lord Latimer's letter to Cromwell. The following day Henry married Jane Seymour.

Was it a week later when Henry presented his new bride to the Court that Katharine Parr first met Thomas Seymour, one of the new queen's brothers? Thomas Seymour enjoyed the favour of his royal brother-in-law in a high degree,and was the handsomest and most admired bachelor of the Court. He has been described as 'fierce in courage, courtly in fashion, in person stately, in voice magnificent, but somewhat empty in matter.' He served his apprenticeship as a seaman and would rise to High Admiral of England.

Parliament dissolved on July 17th, and the Latimers returned to Snape.

It was as if fate was dealing out the cards against the king, for on July 22nd, his illegitimate son, Henry Fitzroy died. He was the natural son of the king from one of his youthful affairs with Elizabeth Blount, a Lady-in-waiting to Catherine of Aragon. The king acknowledged him and gave him the best possible education under Richard Croke,a famous Greek scholar, and John Palsgrave, the author of the first French Grammar in the English language. Fitzroy became a fine horseman and a good musician. In 1525 the king assigned Sheriff Hutton Castle,near York,as a residence for the six year old and created the boy Duke of Richmond, [which relates to Richmond in Yorkshire].

Other titles were added: a Knight of the Garter, Lord High Admiral, Warden of the Cinque Ports,King's Lieutenant General of the North; and Warden of the Scottish Marches. It is believed that the king had thoughts of making him King of Ireland. Plans were made to marry the youthful Henry to foreign princesses, but in 1533 he married Mary Howard, daughter of the third Duke of Norfolk by his second marriage, and sister of the Earl of Surrey. He saw Anne Boleyn executed, and died at the age of seventeen, amid rumours that he had been poisoned by Anne Boleyn and her brother, Lord Rochford. Henry Fitzroy was buried in the church of St. Michael, Framlington, Suffolk.

Early in 1536, Thomas Legh and Richard Layton, agents of Thomas Cromwell, arrived in Yorkshire to begin their investigations into the monasteries. They deposed William Thirsk, Abbot of Fountains Abbey, denouncing, him as a thief, and charging him with immorality, perjury and mismanagement. In the middle of January they set off north from York. The entries in the report give the name of the religious house visited,

16

Gainsborough Old Hall

Gainsborough Old Hall

Snape Hall

Church of St.Michael the Archangel, Well.

the name of the original founder and of the current, and the distance from the last place visited, viz:

Item. to Yedingham, nuns of St.Benedict order, of the foundation of Lord Latymer three miles from the aforesaid place.

Item. to Keldholme, nuns of Cistercian order, of the foundation of Lord Westmorland ten miles from the aforesaid place.

Scandalous stories were told of evil and corrupt practices which were said to take place in the monasteries. Some of them may have had an element of truth, but were difficult to defend. Most likely the monasteries were regarded as hot beds for the support of the Pope, and the king and others had their eyes on the wealth of treasure which the monasteries contained. Other evidence compiled by Cromwell's agents led to the monastic houses worth less than £200 per annum being dissolved and their property confiscated. There were some 376 houses in total, and of these, 53 were in Yorkshire. The loss of the monasteries was a great blow to many country people, especially the poor, who had received succour from the monks and nuns.

The result of all these extreme measures was 'The Pilgrimage of Grace', which was to cause Katharine much anguish and danger, and to present Lord Latimer with the possibility of losing his head! The rising began in Lincolnshire, at Louth, on October 2nd,1536. A commissioner and bishop's chancellor were seized by an excited mob. Gathering momentum, by the time they reached Lincoln there were 40,000 men, 16,000 of whom were armed. A petition was sent to the king asking for the restoration of the monasteries, that the church should be freed from the paying of first-fruits and tenths, that the old holy days should be observed, that the new bishops and Cromwell, together with certain other officials should be dismissed, and that the king should ask for no more money except for the defence of the realm. On October 11th the king sent an insulting reply, refusing to grant their demands.

19

Katharine's stepson, Lord Borough, had his house at Gainsborough threatened by the Lincolnshire mob.

The outbreak in Yorkshire was a much more serious affair, led by Robert Aske, a Yorkshireman who was practicing as a lawyer in London. Some of the nobles who were Roman Catholics joined of their own accord, but others were forced into it by 'the commons'. A rising in Kendal began on October 14th, the townsmen joining in, but not the gentry. Richard Knevet, the father-in-law of Katharine's kinsman Walter Strickland, was approached, but he advised them not to meddle and not to harm Kendal. The rebels replied:'If ye cannot rule, we will!' Among the gentry who assembled at Kendal tollbooth was young Walter Strickland.

Lord Latimer and Sir Christopher Danby were 'taken by the commons' in mid-October and the first despatches from the north reported that they were 'sore constrained'. On October 17th, however, Sir Bryan Hastings wrote to the Earl of Shrewsbury that Lords Latimer and Scrope were 'sworn to the rebels'. Certainly Lord Latimer was advising Robert Aske in late-November at Doncaster at a meeting with the Duke of Norfolk. The king wrote to Norfolk on November 27th:

We desire you to use all good means with Lord Latimer
to induce him to contemn that villain Aske and submit
to our clemancy.

After the amnesty at the end of the year, Lord Latimer went to London to plead his case. He faced a sceptical audience. His defence was that he had been forced to join the rebels and had remained with them in an effort to pesuade them to disband. Cromwell, as we have previously seen, was no friend of Lord Latimer, and regarded him with suspicion. Poor Lord Latimer, on returning north in January 1537, he learned at Stamford Bridge that the commons of Richmondshire:

Grieved at my coming up to London have entered my house at Snape and will destroy it if I come not home shortly. If I do not please them I know not what they will do with my body and goods, wife and children.......If it were the king's pleasure that I might live in such small lands as I have in the south, I would litlle care for my lands in the north.

Cromwell remained unconvinced of Lord Latimer's innocence, but could find nothing concrete against him. He did, however, humiliate his lordship by confiscating the Charterhouse dwelling, forcing him to beg for it back.

It was Katharine's uncle, Sir William Parr, who was charged with delivering Robert Aske to York, Robert Constable to the Duke of Norfolk at Hull, and Sir John Hussey to the Duke of Suffolk at Lincoln. For his part in helping to crush the rebellion, Sir William Parr was granted Lord Lumley's manors.

There was a further rising in Yorkshire which was led by the young Sir Francis Bigod of Settrington. On January 10th,1537, Bigod met John Hallam at Warter Priory. It was arranged that Hallam would attack Hull, and Bigod, with the help of Lord Lumley's son, George, would assault Scarborough. Hallam entered Hull with twenty followers, but received no support from the citizens. The Scarborough venture met with no success either. The king would show no mercy now to any of the rebels; he decreed:

Before you close your banner again you shall cause such dreadful execution to be done upon a good number of these habitants of every town and village that hath offended in this rebellion as by the hanging of them on trees as by the quartering of them and the setting up of their heads in every town great and small which we require you to do without pity or respect.

In 1538, Katharine's sister, Anne, was married in London to William Herbert, a King's Esquire. Her friends Joan Champernoun and Joan Guildford were also married, the former to Anthony Denny, a

Gentleman of the Privy Chamber, and the latter to Sir John Dudley, later Viscount Lisle.

Lord Latimer was serving as a magistrate at York and witnessed three executions, including a woman found guilty of treason. For the rest of the year Katharine and her husband were left in peace at Snape. Latimer was fortunate that he did not suffer any serious consequences for his part in the Pilgrimage of Grace. It has been suggested that the fact that Sir William Parr was such a good servant to the king which saved Lord Latimer from further persecution. In any event, Lord Latimer was granted the nunnery of Nun Monkton, near York.

King Henry had a son now, born the previous year, but at the cost of losing his beloved Jane Seymour. Prince Edward had been born by Caesarian operation. Katharines sister was present at the Christening.

The new Pope made Reginald Pole a cardinal and gave him a mission to try and bring about a reconciliation with the king. Pole had more sense than to come to England, and the Pope did not want to lose him, so he was instructed to go to France or Flanders as the nearest safe point. Needless to tell, Henry's reply was in the negative and also was insulting. Cardinal Pole thought the time must be ripe for a rising in England and that the Tudors could be replaced by the descendants of the Plantagenets. Michael Throgmorton voluntered to go to Rome as a spy for Cromwell. He got the confidence of Pole and became the cardinal's secretary. At first he mislead Cromwell by giving false reports and revealed to Pole many scandals. It was not until later that he threw off his duplicity and wrote to Cromwell with factual information.

Henry Courtney, the Marquis of Exeter, had traitors among his domestic staff who had warned that the Marquis was meditating some secret plans for a rising in the west country. Courtney was arrested, to be followed by the capitulation of Sir Geoffrey Pole, the cardinal's younger brother. Sir Geoffrey, to save his own neck, betrayed the rest. He named his brother, Lord Henry Montague, the Marquis and Marchioness of Exeter, Sir Edward Neville, who closely resembled the king in his appearance, and others.

Exeter, Montague and Neville were sent to the Tower in November. Lady Exeter followed with her companion, Constance Beverley, who had accompanied her on a secret visit to the Nun of Kent. Sir Geoffrey Pole was found guilty along with four others, so was Sir Nicholas Carew, Master of the Horse. Sir Geoffrey received a pardon for his evidence against his compatriots. On December 9th,1538, the Marquis of Exeter, Lord Montague and Sir Edward Neville were beheaded on Tower Hill. Henry Pole's little son disappeared in the Tower. Courtney's youngest son remained a prisoner until Queen Mary ascended the throne in 1553. Early in 1539, Pole's old mother, the Countess of Salisbury was arrested and taken to the Tower. Thus was the danger of a Plantagenet succession removed.

All of the foregoing must have been of great concern to Lord Latimer and Katharine. Thomas Cromwell was still uncertain of Lord Latimer's innocence regarding the Pilgrimage of Grace. Doubtless the faithfulness to the king of Sir William Parr and that Katharine's sister, Anne, was now a courtier and married to Sir William Herbert, who was one of the king's closest companions, saved Lord Latimer.

According to some papers of the Throckmorton family, it seems that Katharine had quite some influence with the king as early as 1540. Sir George Throckmorton,the husband of Katharine Parr's aunt,having incurred the ill-will of Thomas Cromwell, in consequence of some disputes relating to boundaries of their manors of Coughton Court and Ouseley, Cromwell endeavoured to accomplish the ruin of his aristocratic neighbour by accusing him of denying the king's supremacy. The documents of his family show that Sir George was released through the influence of his kinswoman Katharine Parr, and advised with by the king, at her suggestion, about Cromwell, immediately before the arrest of that minister, which was in June of that year. Cromwell was beheaded on July 28th.

Henry had a new queen, Ann of Cleaves. He had not met her before her arrival in England, but she had been represented to him as attractive and he had seen a flattering picture of her. When he saw her in the flesh, he was sorely disappointed. He was angry with Cromwell, who had misrepresented her to him, and he was furious with Hans Holbein, the portrait painter, whom he said had overflattered her. When he saw her he called her a 'Flanders Mare.' Henry declared the marriage null on July 12th, and the bill for the divorce was introduced and processed with great haste.

On July 28th, Henry married Catherine Howard, a girl of some eighteen years and daughter of Lord Edmund Howard, a poverty-stricken noble. Catherine had been appointed as Maid of honour to Anne of Cleaves. The wedding was held in private.

In April of 1541, five priests and a few knights and squires rose in arms in Yorkshire. They were led by Sir John Neville, a member of a lesser branch of the Neville family. They achieved nothing and the movement was immediately crushed without the loss of life, except for the insurgents, who were sent to London, tried and paid with their lives. Sir John Neville suffered at York. This gave Henry the excuse to end the life of the Countess of Salisbury, whom, the reader may recall, had been languishing in the Tower of London for more than a year. She was beheaded on Tower Green, her last words being: 'Blessed are those who suffer persecution for righteousness' sake.'

In the late summer King Henry made a progress to the North of England, bringing his new queen Catherine and a considerable armed force with him. He travelled up through Lincolnshire by a carefully chosen route that ran through the districts affected by the rising of 1536. The king stayed at Gainsborough Hall, the home of Katharine Parr's stepson, Lord Borough. It is possible that he may have held a Council meeting at the hall, for it was his practice to hold them *en route*. He received gifts of money from penitent citizens; at Stamford he was given £20; at Boston £50; at Lincoln £40. The people of Kesteven gave him £50; those of Lindsey £300.

The citizens of York had shown themselves to be unruly, rebellious, perhaps even traitorous: little wonder that they regarded Henry's approach with great anxiety. The streets were to be cleansed, and Coney Street, which was called *King's Street,* was to be paved at the expense of the city. At Micklegate Bar a scaffold was erected from which a speech of welcome would be made. Henry spoiled their plans by entering the city, not by Micklegate Bar, but through Fulford. A speech of submission, most ingratiating in the extreme, was delivered which the king must have listened to with scornful disdain. He did, however, accept the cup of silver, double-gilt, and filled with £100 in gold and one with £40 for his consort.

One of the king's reasons for visiting York was in the hopes of meeting the king of Scotland, his nephew; but the Scottish king declined the invitation. Henry hung on for a few days in the hope that his nephew would arrive, spending his time giving orders as to the future business of the Council of the North, and inspecting the *Minster* and parish churches. In some of the churches he found ancient shrines, still intact, and ordered Edward Lee, Archbishop, to destroy or remove them. He left York on September 26th, calling at Home, Leconfield

Danby Castle

Sinnington : The Old Hall

26

and Hull, before crossing the Humber on his way back to London. Arrived at *Hampton Court,* the king was given information that the queen had had relations with other men. Henry was dumbfounded and sorely distressed. He wept openly in front of his councilmen. The queen confessed to the charges and she was confined to three rooms in *Sion House.* Francis Derham and Thomas Culpepper, the two named in the accusation were tried before a special commission at Guildhall, and hanged at Tyburn on December 13th.

Lord Latimer was summoned to Parliament on January 16th, 1542. In the first days of the session a bill of attainder was brought against Catherine Howard and Lady Rochfort. The bill was passed in the House of Lords on February 11th, in the presence of the Commons. The queen was executed on the 13th.

Was Lord Latimer feeling ill, or was it that he foresaw danger in Scotland? In any event he signed his will on October 1st, after which he was at Berwick-on-Tweed with the invading army of 20,000 men led by the Duke of Norfolk. They pursued a scorched earth policy, destroying all in their path, crops, towns, villages and abbeys. Thinking the job done, Norfolk withdrew his men to York. He had reckoned without the courage of the Scots, who reforming, took the remainder of the English by surprise and caused the rout of the Solway Moss.

Worldly men say that all this came about by misorder and fortune [said John Knox, the famous preacher], but whoever has the least spunk of the knowlege of God, may as evidently see the work of His hand in this discomfiture as ever was seeen in any of the battles left to us in register by the Holy Ghost.

Early in November, Lord Latimer was summoned to London and told to bring Katharine with him. On March 2nd, he died while still in London. In his will, which was proved on March 15th, he requests to be buried at Well, near Snape. He left to his widow one

27

third of his goods and chattels, 'whether of right she ought so to have or not,' all his goods 'now withyn her lying chamber', some plate, one manor in Northamtonshire, £60 of rent at Beoley,Worcestershire. 100 marks and a reversionary interest in his Yorkshire manors of Nun Monkton and Hammerton, after his daughter Margaret.

It would seem that Katharine had met Thomas Seymour before the death of Lord Latimer. To Katharine, who had been married to two husbands in the late years of their lives, this dashing, lithe, swaggering young man of a Seymour must have seemed an exiting challenge. Katharine herself did not seem to be a beauty, she has been described as small and positively made,with thick eyebrows, and a frank, cheerful, florid countenance. At thirty years of age, she was past the meridian of life. Thomas Seymour, like many of the men of his time, was on the make. After all, Katharine's father had been, and so were her uncle and her brother. No doubt Seymour saw her as a steppingstone to higher things. He had reappeared at Court in February 1543 after some months abroad as an observer in the war against the Turks. He pressed his attentions on Katharine and she eventually responded favourably.

In her house in London, Katharine was visited by some of the leading reformers,such as Miles Coverdale, who had made an English translation of the Bible; Hugh Latimer, Bishop of Worcester, and others. Religious assemblies were held there with daily sermons. It was during this period that Katharine became converted to the Protestant faith. Lord Latimer had been a zealous supporter of Roman Catholicism, but now Katharine found herself at liberty to listen to the impassioned eloquence of the apostles of the Reformation.

But if Katharine's heart was set on marrying Thomas Seymour, she was doomed to disappointment,for in the spring of the year, the king made known to her that he wanted her to be his sixth wife. Her affection for Seymour made her very apathetic about the royal marriage at first, but her favoured lover presumed not to contest the prize with his all-powerful brother-in-law and sovereign. A risk of Henry's temper, who held the heads of wives, kinsmen and favourites as cheaply as tennis-balls was not to be withstood. Of course, Katharine, putting on as brave and cheerful a face as possible could do no other than agree, although she did ask the king to wait two months, out of respect for her deceased lord. Thomas Seymour was appointed ambassador to the Queen Regent in Brussells and left the country at the end of April. After that he was almost continuously abroad or at sea, until the last few months of King Henry's reign.

THE ROYAL MARRIAGE

HENRY VIII had come to the throne at the age of eighteen on a wave of popularity, flinging himself into a life of sport and pleasure. During his father's lifetime he had been kept out of the limelight to a great extent, engaging in sport and studies. John Skelton, the Poet Laurette, was his first tutor. He was tall and splendidly built, with glowing auburn hair, combed short and straight in the French fashion. In 1519 he was described as 'much handsomer than the king of France, very fair and his whole frame admirably proportioned. He was a first class horseman and could stay in the saddle for long hours; he exceeded in hawking, wrestling, dancing, archery and sword-play. He also enjoyed jousting and tilting. He was a musician and composed many tunes.

By 1543, Henry was lonely and embittered. Frustrated at being unable to father boys as easily as he could girls, he treated his daughters Mary and Elizabeth with disdain. His lavish lifestyle and self indulgence had made him corpulent and he had suffered a bad fall from his horse whilst jousting in 1536, which caused ulcers on his legs, one of which became chronic.

The arrangements for the royal nuptials were made with a celerity truly astounding; barely four months intervened between the proving of Lord Latimer's will, and the day when Katharine exchanged her widow's weeds for the bridal robes of a queen of England – robes that had proved fatal trappings to four of her five predecessors in the perilous dignity to which it was the pleasure of her enamoured sovereign to advance her. The wedding rites of Henry and Katharine, instead of being hurried over secretly in an obscure corner, like some unhallowed mystery (as was the case with his previous marriages with Anne Boleyn and Catherine Howard), were solemnized much in the same manner as royal marriages in the 19th century, without pageantry, but with all suitable observances, and duly attested by a notary:

Witnesseth that on the 12 July 1543, 35 Henry VIII, in an upper oratory called the Queen's privy closet within the honour of Hampton Court, Westminster Diocese, in the presence of noble and gentle persons named at the foot of this instrument and of me Richard Watkins, the King's prothonotary; the King and Lady Katharine Latimer, alias Parr being met there for the purpose of solemnising matrimony between them, Stephen Bishop of Winchester [Gardiner] proclaimed in England that they were met to join in marriage the said king and Lady Katharine, and if anyone knew of any impediment thereto he should declare it. -----

The license for the marriage without banns, sealed by Cranmer dated 10 July 1543 being then brought in and none opposing but all applauding the marriage, the said Bishop of Winchester put the question to which the King replied,'hilari vulta' (yea) and the Lady Katharine also replied that it was her wish. And then the King, taking her right hand, repeated after the Bishop the words: 'I,Henry,take thee, Katharine, to my wedded wife, to have and to hold from this day forward, for better, for worse, for richer,for

poorer,in sickness and in health, till death us depart and thereto
I plight thee my troth.'

Then releasing and again clasping hands,the Lady Katharine likewise said: 'I Katharine, take thee, Henry, to my wedded husband,
to have and to hold from this day forward, for better for worse,
for richer for poorer, in sickness and in health. To be bonair and
buxome in bed and at board, till death us depart and thereto I
plight thee my troth.'

The putting on of the wedding ring and the proffer of gold and
silver followed; and the Bishop, after a prayer, pronounced a
benediction. The King then commanded the prothonotary to make a
public instrument of the premises.

Present: Lord Russell,K.G. Keeper of the Privy Seal. Sir Anthony
Browne,K.G. Captain of the King's Pensioners, Thomas Henneage,
Edward Seymour (Earl of Hertford), Henry Knyvett, Richard Long,
Thomas Darcy, Edward Boynton, and Thomas Speke. Knights.
Anthony Denny and William Herbert, Esquires.
The ladies Mary and Elizabeth [the king's daughters]
Katherine, Duchess of Suffolk, Anne, Countess of Hertford, Joan
Lady Dudley.
and
Anne Herbert.

The last named was,of course,Katharine Parr's sister.
The Duchess of Suffolk was the former Katherine Willoughby, a friend of long standing to Katharine Parr.
The Countess of Hertford [Edward Seymour's wife] was
the former Joan Guildford.

Katharine presented her royal step-daughter and
bridesmaid, Princess Mary, with a magnificent pair of
gold bracelets set with rubies, and the gift in money of
£25. Of course the Princess Elizabeth, who also
assisted at the bridal was not forgotten.

Preparations were made in the week following the
wedding for the annual Summer Progress, which was a
gentle one from Surrey, through Buckinghamshire and
Bedfordshire. In Oatland, Surrey, Katharine wrote to
her brother, William:

31

It having pleased God to incline the king to take me as his wife, which is the greatest joy and comfort that could happen to me, I inform you as the person who has the most cause to rejoice thereat; and require you to let me sometimes hear of your health as friendly as if I had not been called to this honour.

Given at my Lord's manor of Oatlands.

20th July 35 Henry VIII.

Addressed to my well-beloved brother, the Lord Parr,

Lord Warden of the Marches.

Putting aside all thoughts of Thomas Seymour, the queen entered into her new marriage in her usual dutiful and loving way. She became a caring stepmother to the princesses Mary and Elizabeth and the young Prince Edward.

A sour note sounded from Anne of Cleaves, who said that Katharine was not so young and pretty as herself, and declared that she: 'would like to be in her shirt, so to speak, with her mother, having especially taken great grief and despair at the king's espousal of this last wife, who is not nearly so beautiful as she, besides that there is no hope of issue, seeing that she had none with her two former husbands'.

There was great rejoicing at the University of Cambridge at the union of the sovereign with the pious and learned Lady Latimer. At Cambridge the doctrines of the Reformation had taken deep root already. A congratulatory address was sent to the king. Katharine continued to correspond with the university, in the name of which the celebrated Roger Ascham thanked her for her royal benefactions and the suavity of her letters.

Write to us oftener, most learned queen, and do not despise the term erudition, most noble lady: it is the praise of your industry, and a greater one to your talents than all the ornaments of your fortune. We rejoice vehemently in your happiness, most happy princess! because you are learning more amidst the occupations of your dignity,than many of us do in all our leisure and quiet.

32

Katharine's attachment to the doctrines of the Reformation made her a jealous enemy in Stephen Gardiner, the leader of the anti-papal Henrican party: and as early as the second week after her marriage, this audacious churchman dared to challenge the power of the royal bride, by an attack on an humble society of Reformers at Windsor. Anthony Parsons, a priest, John Marbeck, a chorister and musician, Robert Testwood and Henry Filmer were the leading persons attached to this community, but it was suspected that they received encouragement from members of the royal household. A few manuscript notes and a Latin Concordance in progress of compilation, which were found in the house of Marbeck furnished an excuse for the arrest, trial and condemnation of himself and his three friends. Nothing could induce them to betray any person in the royal household, to save themselves from the fiery death with which they were threatened. The king granted Marbeck a reprieve, through his love of music, but the other three were burned at the stake on July 26th, two days after being sentenced. Though the flames of their martyrdom were kindled almost within sight of Henry's Protestant queen, she was unable to save the victims; and well aware was she that the blow which produced this cruel sacrifice of human life was aimed at herself, and would be followed by an attack on persons in her immediate confidence. Such were the events in the honeymoon month of the new queen.

Katharine's elevation to the dangerous dignity of queen consort afforded her, however, the satisfaction of advancing the fortunes of members of her own family. She bestowed the office of Lord Chamberlain on her uncle, Lord Parr of Horton; she made her sister, Lady Herbert, one of the Ladies of her Bedchamber; and her step-daughter Margaret Neville, she appointed one of her maids of honour.

The king was in a good humour for he had signed a treaty with the Scots and the young Mary was crowned Queen of Scotland at Stirling in the autumn. The Scottish nobles, however, put an end to the treaty by the end of the year.

Katharine set about establishing a royal nursery for her step-children and they were all at home with their father for Christmas. Katharine chose tutors of wide culture and humanist inclinations, who like herself, had been influenced by the teachings of Desiderious Erasmus, such as John Cheke, who became tutor to Prince Edward; he was one of the few people of whom the prince was fond. Cheke also taught the princess Elizabeth. Other teachers were Anthony Cooke and William Grindall.

It would seem that Katharine herself had a hand in the tutoring of Prince Edward, most likely teaching him to write, for a great similarity has been noticed in his handwriting to that of the queen's.

The king was becoming more corpulent than ever, eating and drinking to excess. Consequently, in March 1544, the ulcer on his thigh flared up again and he was stricken with a fever. The physicians of the day treated ulcers by keeping them open. Because of his size the king had a special suit of armour made which could accomodate his huge paunch and he managed to wear this when he went on his last expedition to France in July, 1544. Katharine's step-son, John Neville, the new Lord Latimer, now sixteen years of age, went with him. Henry rode on horseback to the siege of Boulogne. Katharine wrote to Henry:

The time seemeth to me very long, with a great desire to know how your Highness hath done since your departing hence; whose prosperity and health I prefer and desire more than mine own. And whereas I know your Majesty's absence is never without great need, yet love and affection compel me to desire your presence. Again the same zeal and affection forceth me to be best

KATHARINE PARR
NATIONAL PORTRAIT GALLERY
Portrait attributed to William Scrots.

35

content with that which is your will and pleasure.

Thus, love maketh me in all things set apart mine own convenience and pleasure and to embrace most joyfully his will and pleasure whom I love. God, the knower of secrets, can judge these words to be not only written with ink but most truly impressed upon the heart.

Henry's replies were brief but amiable: Would write again with his own hand but is so busy.

Is too busy to write more, but sends blessings to all his children and recommendations to his cousin Margaret and the rest of his ladies and gentlewomen and to his Council.

No more to you at this time, sweetheart,but for lack of time and great occupation of business.

Early in the New Year Henry caused his Parliament to settle the royal succession on any children he might have by Katharine, in case Prince Edward died without issue. Several of the queen consorts of England have excercised vice-regal powers, either by usurption or the consent of the sovereign; but Katharine Parr was the first and only one on whom the style and title of Queen Regent was solemnly conferred, and who signed herself as such.

Katharine's regency was conducted with such prudence and careful administration that there could be no cause for complaint. Her last act as regent was to command the Council to issue a general order on September 19th, 'That a public thanksgiving should be offered up to Almighty God in all the towns and villages throughout England, for the taking of Boulogne.'

The king returned to England on October 1st, finding it impossible to follow up on his victorious career in France, because his Spanish allies had made a seperate peace with Francis I, king of France.

The following February Henry's fever returned. We can be sure that Katharine played her part as a loving nurse, but it was apparent to all that he was physically declining. Henry Howard noted: 'whose glutted cheeks sloth feeds so fat, as scant their eyes can be seen.'

In the July the king was at Portsmouth on his flagship the *Great Harry*. During the ensuing naval action he saw the *Mary Rose*, named after his sister, sink. She had been caught with gun portholes open and was swamped. Five hundred men were trapped and all but twenty were drowned. It is said that Henry wept.

Charles Brandon, the Duke of Suffolk, who was commanding one of the armies, died suddenly. Brandon was a long-standing companion of the king and became his brother-in-law when he married Mary Tudor in 1515, which earned him the king's disapproval at the time, although it was said that Brandon was the only man the king ever loved. It was said of Brandon at Court, that no woman could resist his advances. Mary Tudor was his third wife. Lady Willoughby, having run into debt, sold the wardship of her daughter, Katherine, to the Duke of Suffolk. He had intended to marry the girl to his young son, the Earl of Lincoln, but when Brandon was fortynine and finding himself a widower, he espoused the fourteen year old Katherine himself.

Katharine Parr's reputation as a scholar and theologian, did not make her neglectful of the skills of needlework, in which she much delighted. She employed her hours of retirement in embroidering among her ladies. It is said that a portion of the tapestry which hung in the royal apartments in the Tower of London, before they were dismantled or destroyed, were the work of Katharine.

Her taste in dress appears to have been of a high standard, combining luscious materials with simplicity of form. In fact she enacted her role as queen with as much splendour as any of her predecessors. The Spanish ambassador gave a description of her wearing apparel as he observed her at a grand festival in the Palace of Westminster:

37

She wore a kirtle of brocade, and an open robe of cloth of gold; the sleeves lined with crimson satin, and trimmed with three-piled crimson velvet; the train more than two yards long. Suspended from the neck were two crosses, and a jewel of very rich diamonds; in her head dress, also, were many rich and beautiful ones. Her girdle was of gold, with very large pendants.

Katharine also found time to write a little book, *Lamentations of a sinner.* This little volume, next to the writing of Sir Thomas More, affords one of the finest specimens of English composition of that era. Within the limits of some 120 minature pages, it comprises the substance of almost all the sermons that have been levelled against Papal supremacy. The authoress compliments Henry for having released England from that domination. Katharine also wrote a little book of prayers, executed in a miniature size and bound in a silver casing. The original volume is kept in the Mayor's Parlour at Kendal.

Katharine continued to pursue the opinions of the religion to which she had become a convert and urged Henry to keep pressing ahead with the Reformation. She appointed Miles Coverdale as her almoner, giving him every assistance. Nicholas Udall, the learned master of Eton school, she engaged to edit the translations of Eramus's *Paraphrases on the four Gospels.* in which Princess Mary was encouraged by Katharine, to take an active share. The first edition of this work was published in 1545, at the sole expense of the queen.

Intellectually she could hold her own with the king and at first he enjoyed their discussions. There is no doubt she was able to influence him in many ways. She was instrumental in saving Cambridge University, when that ancient seat of learning was threatened.

Henry was by now so gross and unwieldly, his body swollen with dropsy, that it was impossible for him to take exercise. Machinery had to be used to lift him into the upper chambers. These limitations did nothing to improve his disposition, the king's severity to his subjects continued as forceful as ever. His physical disabilities increased his natural irascibility to such a degree, that scarcely any of his domestics approached him without terror. The disorder in his leg had now grown extremely painful; and this added to his monstrous corpulency, which made it difficult to stir, made him more furious than a chained lion.

Katharine was the most skilful and patient of nurses. She did not shrink from performing any act which would alleviate Henry's suffering. It is recorded that she would remain for hours on her knees beside him, applying fomentations and other palliatives to his ulcerated thigh, which he would not permit anyone to dress but her.

The beginning of the year 1546, saw the last great spectacle of royal festivity and splendour, when the diplomatic envoys arrived to negotiate a peace between England and France. Henry presented Katharine with many jewels of great value that she might cut a brilliant figure, as his consort, to the French diplomats. He also provided new and costly drapes and furnishings for her apartments, as well as plate.

Henry peremtorily put an end to these negotiations to end his war with France and sent the mediators home deeply disappointed. However, in the summer there was peace between England and France.

Evil forces were at work behind Katharine's back. John Lassells, who informed on Catherine Howard, was arrested for heresy; so was the preacher Edward Crome, Hugh Latimer and Nicholas Shaxton, Bishop of Salisbury. Also apprehended was Anne Askew, a woman 'very obstinate and heady in matters of religion.' She had been arrested on two occasions in the previous year, but proved to have influential friends at Court. Anne, who was a Protestant, was first of all prompted to involve people who were most likely innocent. She was found guilty after a terrible interrogation by Bishop Gardiner. Anne Askew lived long enough to write her own account of her experiences in the Tower of London with Sir Richard Rich and Sir Thomas Wriothsley, the new Lord Chancellor.

Then Master Rich sent me to the Tower, where I remained till three o'clock, when Rich and one of the Council came charging me upon my obedience to show them if I knew any man or any woman of my sect. Answered that I knew none. Then they asked me of my lady of Suffolk, my lady of Sussex, my lady Hertford, my lady Denny and my lady Fitzwilliam. Answered that if I should pronounce anything against them I could not prove it.

Then they said the King was informed that I could name, if I would, a great number of my sect.

Answered that the King was well deceived in that behalf as dissembled with in other matters.'

[But she had needed money to pay for food in the Tower; divers ladies had sent her money].

I answered that there was a man in a blue coat who delivered me ten shillings and said my lady of Hertford sent it to me; and another in a violet coat gave me eight shillings, and said my lady Denny sent it to me: whether it were true or not, I cannot tell; for I am not sure who sent it me, but as the maid did say.

Then they said, there were of the Council that did maintain me; and I said No.

Then they did put me on the rack, because I confessed no ladies or gentlemen to be of my opinion, and thereon they kept me a long time; and because I lay still, and did not cry, my lord Chancellor and Master Rich took pains to rack me with their own hands, till I was nigh dead.

Then the lieutenant caused me to be loosed from the rack. Incontinently I swooned, and then they recovered me again.

After that I sat two long hours reasoning with my lord Chancellor upon the bare floor; where he, with many flattering words persuaded me to leave my opinion. But my Lord God (I

40

thank his everlasting goodness) gave me grace to persevere, and I will do, I hope, to the very end.

The poor woman was burned to death at Smithfield on July 16th, mainly for denouncing the mass. John Lassells was one of the other heretics who suffered.

The writing was on the wall now. Anne Askew was a lady of noble birth and ancient ancestry, and having become a convert to the new faith, was for that reason violently driven from her home by her husband, a Mr. Kyne of Lincolnshire. She resumed her maiden name and devoted herself to the cause of the new religion. It was soon known that the queen's sister, Lady Herbert; the Duchess of Suffolk, and other great ladies of the Court, encouraged her; even the queen herself had received books from her, in the presence of Lady Herbert, Lady Tyrwhitt, and the youthful Lady Jane Gray, which might bring her majesty under the penalty of the statute against reading heretical works. The supposed connection of the 'fair gospeller', as she was known, with the queen caused her to be singled out for the purpose of terrifying or torturing her into confessions that might provide a charge of heresy or treason against her royal mistress. But if Anne had been helped by any of the ladies mentioned, she was too strong, even under the torment of the rack, to disclose their interest in her.

Some said that Henry was getting restless. Katharine had shown no signs of bearing him children, and there were those who said he had his eye on the young widow of the Duke of Suffolk, his brother-in-law, the former Katherine Willoughby.

Queen Katharine had been accustomed of an evening to converse privately with the king on religious subjects, in which he took great delight. The points of difference in their opinions, and the ready wit and eloquence with which the queen was able to sustain her case gave spice and stimulation to these arguments. Henry was at first amused and intrigued; but contentions between husband and wife are dangerous pastimes, the more so if the wife gets the best of the argument. When the queen brought the discussion round to the recent trials, the king suddenly became furious and abruptly ended the discussion. As they were in the company of Gardiner, the king being confined to his chamber with an agravated inflamation of his ulcer, which did nothing to improve his temper; Katharine reading a danger signal, made a few pleasant remarks on other subjects and withdrew.

'A good hearing it is,' said the king to Gardiner,'when women become such clerks; and much to my comfort to come, in mine old age, to be taught by my wife!'

Gardiner must have been delighted at the King's reaction and he took advantage of the situation to insinuate things against her majesty, which a few days before, he would never for fear of his life have breathed to the king. The monster in Henry flared up. Forgotten now all the tender care with which Katharine had nursed him, her attentions to his every comfort, together with her amiable and affectionate conduct to his children. He allowed Gardiner to have articles drawn up against the queen. Wriothsley, in carrying the documents from the king's chamber, after obtaining his signature, accidentally dropped the papers from his clothing, where he had concealed them, in the gallery at Whitehall. They were picked up by a member of the queen's staff. When the queen was informed she went into hysterics and made such a commotion that the king sent his personal physician to her aid, and later paid her a visit himself, having to be carried in his chair to her chamber, 'where compassionating her estate, he used such kind words as did help recover her.'

Shortly after, attended by Lady Herbert, her sister, Katharine went to the king's bedchamber. He welcomed

Katharine Parr
Reproduction by kind permission of His Grace
the Archbishop of Canterbury. Copyright
reserved to the Church Commissioners and
the Courtauld Institute of Art.

43

Katharine Parr (1547)

her courteously and began to talk of religion, but the queen had learned to be cautious and was not going to fall into that trap.She declared that she 'was but a woman, accompanied therefore, in all matters of doubt and difficulty, she must refer herself to his majesty's better judgement, as to her lord and head; for so God hath appointed you as the supreme head of us all, and of you, next unto God, will I ever learn.'

'Not so, by Saint Mary!' exclaimed the king, 'Ye are become a doctor Kate, to instruct us, and not to be instructed of us, as oftentimes we have seen.'

'Indeed,' replied the queen, 'if your majesty have so conceived, my meaning has been mistaken, for I have always held it prespoterous for a woman to instruct her lord; and if I have presumed to differ with your highness on religion, it was partly to obtain information for my own comfort, regarding certain nice points on which I stood in doubt, and sometimes because I perceived that, in talking, you were better able to pass away the pain and weariness of your present infirmaty, which encouraged me to this boldness, in the hope of profiting withal by your majesty's learned discourse.'

'And is it so, sweetheart?' returned the king; 'then we are perfect friends.' He then kissed her with tenderness, and gave her leave to depart. He forgot all about the warrant.

On the day that had been appointed for her arrest, the king being in a slightly improved state of health, he was able to walk out in the garden with the queen. Katharine was attended by Lady Jane Gray, her sister, Lady Herbert and Lady Tyrwhitt, her step-daughter. Presently the Lord Chancellor Wriothsley, with forty of the guard, entered the garden with the intention of arresting the queen and taking her to the Tower. The king, suddenly remembering that he had signed a warrant for the queen's arrest, burst out in indignation: 'Beast! Fool! Nave!' and sternly withdrawing him from the earshot of the queen, he bade him 'avaunt from his presence.'

Katharine, when she saw the king in such a fury with his chancellor had the grace to intercede on his behalf. 'Ah, poor soul!' said the king, 'Thou little knowest, Kate, how evil he deserveth this grace at thy hands. On my word, sweetheart, he hath been to thee a very knave!'

During the last quarter of 1546, the king had a series of ups and downs with his health. He was able to go to Oatlands, but fell ill there about December 10th. Katharine had been sent to Greenwich for Christmas when Henry returned to London. The Court was closed to all except the Privy Council and some gentlemen of the Chamber. It soon became apparent to all who saw him that the king was in his final decline. On Boxing Night, the king called for Hertford, Dudley, Paget, Denny and two others. He asked Denny to bring his will. At first Denny produced an earlier document, but when they started to read it to him, Henry said:'That was not it, but there was another of a later making, written with the hand of Lord Wriothsley, being Secretary.' The will in question was then found and when it was read out Henry said he wished to make some alterations to it. He told Paget: 'To put in some that were not named before, and to put out the Bishop of Winchester's name.' He also asked Paget to remove Stephen Gardiner's name, saying, 'He was a wilful man and not meet to be about his son, and that the Bishop of Westminster should be put out also, because he was schooled by the Bishop of Winchester.' They pleaded with the king to restore Gardiner, but he would not relent. 'He marvelled what we meant and that we all knew him as a wilful man, that Gardiner should not be about his son, nor trouble his Council any more.'

The will was sealed four days later, the king being too weak to actually sign the document.

46

In early January the king was gravely ill. Neither Katherine or Princess Mary were allowed into his chamber. On the 27th of the month it was clear that he was sinking beyond hope of recovery, but who was going to tell him? Even the doctors were too afraid of losing their heads for forecasting the king's death, as poor Lord Hungerford had done six years earlier.It was Anthony Denny who finally took the bull by the horns and told the king that he must prepare himself for his final agony. Denny asked him if he wanted any churchman to minister to him. The king replied that if he did want anyone, it would be Cranmer, but he would have a little sleep first, then see how he felt, and would then advise upon the matter. After an hour or two he awoke and asked for Cranmer who was at that time at Croydon. By the time the archbishop had been sent for and arrived on the spot, the king was speechless.

Although rendered mute, Henry was still conscious and Cranmer asked him to give some sign that he put his trust in God through Jesus Christ. The king,'holding him with his hand, did wring his hand in his as hard as he could.'

Such was the end of King Henry VIII. The news of his death was kept secret for three days. On February 14th he was buried, as was his wish, beside Jane Seymour, the mother of the new king.

THE FOURTH MARRIAGE

DID HENRY intend to end his marriage to Katharine Parr? A clause in his will states:

And per default of lawful issue of our son prince Edward, we will that the said imperial crown, and other premises, after our two deceases, shall fully remain and come down to the heirs of our entirely beloved queen Katharyne that now is, or of any other our lawful wife that we shall hereafter marry.

From the last sentence it would seem that he expected to outlive Katharine.However, in the preamble to the legacy, he outlines her virtues:

And for the great love, obedience, chastity of life, and wisdom being our wife and queen, we bequeath unto her for her proper life, and as it shall please her to order it, three thousand pounds in plate, jewels, and stuff of household goods, and such apparel as it shall please her to take of such as we have already. And further, we give unto her one thousand pounds in money, and the ammount of her dower and jointure according to our grant in parliament.

We remember that the king left two widows, for Anne of Cleaves was still alive, but it was Katharine who was prayed for as queen dowager by her old enemy Gardiner, who offered the following prayer:

'I commend to God queen Katharine, dowager, my lady Mary's grace, and my lady Elizabeth's grace, your majesty's dear sisters.'

The young King Edward VI wrote a letter in Latin, ex pressing his condolence to his widowed stepmother, calling her his 'dear mother', and concluding, 'Farewell, venerated queen.'

During the period of her royal widowhood, Katharine resided in her palace at Chelsea, on the banks of the Thames, with its beautiful and extensive gardens.

As the new king was only a boy of nine, a Protectorate was set up, as per the late king's directions, the chief lord being the young king's uncle, Edward Seymour, Earl of Hertford. The others were the Archbishop of Canterbury, Thomas, Lord Wriothsley, Chancellor of England; William, Lord St.John; John, Lord Russell; John, Viscount Lisle; Cuthbert Tunstal, Bishop of Durham; Anthony Browne, William Paget, Edward North, Edward Montague, Anthony Denny, and William Herbert.

The Protectorate drew up a list of persons for enoblement, for the late king had remarked to Paget that the nobility was in a state of decay. Many peerages had become extinct, 'some by attainder, some by misgovernance and riotous living, some by sickness and other means.' The list consisted of Hertford named for a dukedom, Parr for a marquisate, St.John [John Dudley, later Duke of Northumberland], Lisle and Russell for earldoms, Sir Thomas Seymour, Sir Thomas Cheyne, Sir Richard Rich, Sir William Willoughby, Sir R.Arundel, Sir Edward Sheffield, Sir John St.Leger, Sir - Wymbish, Sir Christopher Danby, and Vernon of the Peak for baronies.

Lord Parr, Katharine's brother, was to be Marquis of Nothampton.

Sir Thomas Seymour should be styled Lord Seymour of Sudely, with 500 lands, and he was created High Admiral of England. He had given good service at sea during the French war. King Henry, although he had not named him among the executors, had given him a place on the Privy Council. Though raised to the peerage, presented with large estates, and with a well-paid and responsible office, he was still dissatisfied with his lot. He demanded the consent of the Council to a marriage with Princess Elizabeth, who was not quite fifteen at the time. The councillors did not feel that he was a fit enough character to take his demand seriously.

Thomas Seymour was suspected of conspiring with pirates. His business with the Admiralty had brought him into contact with privateers. With improvements in navigation there was an expanding world trade and merchant ships were carrying increasingly rich cargoes. The Spanish, French, English, Scottish, and Flemish pirates had through war service learned the art of plundering enemy ships. In peacetime they put their knowledge and skills to illegal use. Fleets of privateers recruited largely from the harbours of Cornwall and Devon, sailing in convoys of twenty and thirty ships, occupied the mouth of the Channel, pillaging Spanish gold ships from Panama, French wine ships from

Bordeaux, the rich traders from Antwerp, or from the Thames. If caught they were handed over to Seymour at the Admiralty and the cargoes that were recovered were supposed to be returned to their rightful owners. Too often complaints were received from the merchants that they did not receive their merchandise, and furthermore, the miscreants went unpunished.

Thomas Seymour was jealous of his brother's power and sought to advance his own career.

The Protector too was ambitious, that he might do great things for the country; his brother's was the ambition of selfishness. The Protector was a religious man; 'the admiral,' said Hugh Latimer, 'was a man furthest from the fear of God that ever he knew or heard of in England.' The Protector's moral life was blameless; the admiral had seduced and deserted at least one innocent woman, who fell into crime and was executed.

Thomas, to pursue his own ends, won the acquaintance of one John Fowler, King Edward's private attendant, and bribed him into enquiring about the possibility of marrying Princess Elizabeth. He asked Fowler if the king did not sometimes enquire after him: 'Then I demanded of him, "What question should his majesty ask of you?" "Nay, nothing, (said he) only sometimes his highness would ask why I married not." "I never heard him ask such a question," quoth I. Then my lord paused for a while, and after said to me, "Mister Fowler, I pray you, if you have any communication with the king's majesty soon, or tomorrow, ask his highness whether he would consent I should marry or not; and if he says he will be content, I pray you ask his grace whom he would have to be my wife?" I said I would and that night, his highness being alone, I said to his majesty, "And please your grace, I marvel my Lord Admiral marrieth not." His highness saying nothing to it, I said again, "Could your grace be

50

contented he should marry?" His grace said,"Yea,very well." Then I asked his majesty whom would that he should marry? His highness said,"My lady Anne of Cleaves," and so pausing awhile, said after, "Nay, nay, wot you what? I would he marry my sister Mary, to turn her opinions." His highness went his ways and said no more at that time.'

Thomas Seymour turned his attention back to Katharine Parr, whom, the reader will recall, he had arranged to marry following the death of Lord Latimer. Katharine was still in love with this swashbuckler of a man and would colour up at the mention of his name. He had the art to make the queen dowager believe that he had remained a bachelor for her sake.

Katharine wrote to Seymour:

I would not have you think that this, mine honest goodwill to-wards you, proceeds from any sudden motion of passion; for, as truly as God is God, my mind was fully bent the other time I was at liberty to marry you before any man I know. Howbeit, God withstood my will therein most vehemenently for a time, and through His grace and goodness made that seem possible which seemed to me most impossible: that was, made me renounce ut-terly mine own will, and follow him most willingly. It were long to write all the process of this matter. If I live I shall declare it to you myself. I can say nothing; but as my lady of Suffolk saith: "God is a marvellous man."

Katharine the Queen.

A clandestine relationship developed, but Katharine bade Thomas wait until two years after Henry's death. Thomas was making visits to the palace at Chelsea during the hours of darkness, as the following letter shows:

My lord, as I gather by you letter, delivered to my brother [in-law] Herbert, ye are in some fear how to frame my lord, your brother to speak in your favour. The denial of your request shall make his folly more manifest to the world, which will more grieve me than the want of his speaking. I would not wish you to importune for his goodwill, if it come not frankly at the first.It shall be sufficient once to require it, and then cease. I would desire you might obtain the king's letter in your favour, and also the aid and furtherance of the most notable of the Council, such as ye shall think convenient; which thing obtained shall be no small shame to your brother and loving sister [in-law] in case they do the like.

My Lord, whereas ye charge me with a promise, written with my own hand, to change two years into two months, I think ye have no such plain sentence written with my hand. I know not whether ye be a paraphraser or not. If ye be learned in that science, it is possible ye may of one word make a whole sentence, and yet not at all times after the true meaning of the writerö as it appeareth by this your exposition upon my writing.

When it shall be your pleasure to repair hither, ye must take some pains to come early in the morning, that ye may be gone again by 7 o'clock; and so I suppose ye may come without suspect. I pray you let me have knowledge over-night at what hour ye will come, that your portress may wait at the gate to the fields for you.

And thus, my most humble and hearty commendations, I take my leave of you for this time, giving ye thanks for your coming to Court when I was there.

from Chelsea.

P.S. I will keep in store till I speak with my lord's large offer of Fausterne, at which time I shall be glad to know your further pleasure therein.

By her that is, and shall be, your humble, true, and loving wife during her life.

     Katharine the Quen. K.P.

From the signing off of this letter it would appear that she and Seymour were already married, albeit without the consent of the king, and in secret. However, we should remember that a promise of marriage was held as binding at that time. It seems out of scharacter with everything else that Katharine had done in her life. She was without doubt, dazzled and infatuated by this

restless, manipulative, scheming man.
Agnes Strickland, in her book *Lives of the Queens of England*, states that one month and three days after the death of King Henry, a written contract of marriage and rings of betrothal were exchanged between Katharine and Seymour, but the nuptials were not solemnized until two months later. Their secret meetings were not so safe as Thomas thought, as the following letter from Thomas to Katharine, written on the 17th May, reveals:

Yesternight, I supped at my brother [in–law] Herbert's, of whom, for your sake besides my own, I received good cheer; and after the same, I received from your Highness, by my sister [in-law] Herbert, your commendations, which were more welcome than they were sent. And after the same, she waded further with me touching upon my lodging with your Highness at Chelsea, Which I denied, but that indeed I went to the garden as I went to the Bishop of London's house, and at that point stood with her a long time, till at last she told me by further tokens, which made me change colour, who, like a false wench, took me with the manner; then remembering what she was, and knowing how well ye trusted her, examined whether those things came from your Highness or were feigned. She answered "that they came from your Highness, and he [Lord Herbert] knew it to be true," for which I render unto your Highness my most humble and hearty thanks, for by her company, in default of yours, I shall shorten the weeks in these parts, which heretofore were four days longer in every one of them than they were under the plummet at Chelsea.

From him whom ye have bound to honour, love and
in all lawful things obey,

T.Seymour & c.

Seemingly the efforts to approach the Council, as advised by the queen, had failed. Seymour was hesitant about tackling the king in person, so again sought the aid of John Fowler to obtain the king's blessing to the marriage. The Court had moved to St.James's Palace

53

Sudely Castle

The Chapel, Sudely Castle

54

and Thomas buttonholed Fowler in the great gallery. Fowler kept him on tenterhooks at first, until Seymour demanded sharply,'Have you done as I bade you?'

Fowler repeated what the king had said about Anne of Cleaves and his sister. Thomas laughed, then said: 'I pray you, Mr Fowler, if you may soon, ask His Grace if he could be contented I should marry the queen – and, in case I be a suitor to His Highness for a letter to the queen, whether His Majesty would write for me or not.' Fowler said he would do so that night.

The king had a strong affection for his uncle Thomas, so he was in agreement with the arrangement. On June 25th, Edward wrote to Katharine:

To the Queen's Grace,

We thank you heartily, not only for the gentle acceptance of our suit unto you, but also for lovingly accomplishing of the same, wherein you have declared, not only a desire to gratify us, but to declare the goodwill, likewise, that we bear to you in all your requests, wherefore ye shall not need to fear any grief to come or suspect lack of aid in need, seeing that he, being my uncle, is of so good a nature that he will not be troublesome any means unto you, and I of such mind, that for divers just causes I must favour you. But even without cause you merely require help against him whom you have put in trust with the carriage of these letters, so may I return the same request unto you, to provide that he may live with you without grief, which hath given him wholly unto you; and I will provide for you both, that if hereafter any grief befall, I shall be a sufficient succour in your Godly and praisable enterprises.

Fare ye well, with much increase in honour and virtue in Christ.

From St.James, the five-and-twenty day of June,

Edward.

From the wording of this letter, it would appear that they had deceived the king into thinking that he himself had made the match.

When Thomas Seymour's brother, the Protector, came

to know of the marriage andthe direct approach to the king, he was furious that his brother had side-stepped the Council and created a *fait accompli*. His rages were alarming to the boy king, who later noted them in his journal. Cranmer had performed the actual ceremony, but there is no record of when it actually took place. The king remained under the impression that the wedding had taken place sometime in May. However, the thing was passed over for the time being, and on the breaking out of the war with Scotland, to cover any unpleasant feelings, the admiral was desired to take command of the fleet; instead he gave the command to Lord Clinton, staying at home himself to manage the Admiralty.

The Protector's wife had long bourne a grudge against Katharine. She considered that in marrying Thomas Seymour, she had married beneath her, and that the duchess herself should take precedence over Katharine. She refused to bear the queen's train, saying that 'it was unsuitable for her to perform that service for the wife of her husband's youngest brother.' Katharine soon invoked the act of Henry VIII, whereby it was provided that Anne of Cleaves should take precedence after his queen and the princesses, his daughters, of every other lady in the realm. That settled the matter, but the duchess still bore her grudge.

The Protector began to take a strict hold on the purse strings of the nation, allowing the king very little pocket money. He also maintained that the jewels given to the queen by King Henry, were the property of the State. Thomas tried to enlist the help of John Fowler once more, offering bribes of pocket money to the king. 'I pray you tell His Grace I would be a suitor to my lord my brother for certain jewels which the king that dead is gave the queen, thinking the law she have them – whereof one is her wedding ring.'

Fowler replied: 'Alas! my lord, that ever jewels, or

56

muck of this world, should make you begin a new matter between my lord's Grace and you.' 'Nay', Seymour assured him, 'there will be no business for this matter, for I trust my brother will be content.' Fowler did not raise this subject with the king, although Seymour was not content to let it rest permanently.

The king complained to the Marquis of Dorset that 'My uncle of Somerset dealeth very hardly with me, and keepeth me so straight that I cannot have money at my will. But my Lord Admiral both sends me money, and gives me money.' During that summer of 1547, the king instructed Fowler to write to the admiral to say how grateful he was and that he would like some money now. When Fowler asked what sum the king had in mind, he replied, 'As it pleaseth his lordship.' Fowler wrote to Seymour informing him that 'His Majesty desireth it for presents, but I cannot tell for whom. I pray your lordship to burn this letter.'

Thomas Seymour was quick to play on the parsimony of his brother and Fowler was used more and more until the admiral could talk to the king in person. He fortold that Somerset's expedition to Scotland would be a failure. Seeing that the object was to secure the little Queen of Scotland for his bride, Thomas's prediction was right in part, for the girl had been transferred to France. Gaining confidence, the admiral tried to raise the matter of the queen's jewels with the king, but the king told him, 'If it is good, the Lords will allow it.If it is ill, I will not write it.' Seymour continued to press: 'The Lords will take it in better part if you will write it.'. Edward said 'Let me alone.' The young king must have felt in a quandary, for he consulted John Cheke, who advised him, 'Ye were best not to write.'

A little while later the admiral came again to the king at Westminster and said, 'You must take it upon yourself to rule, for ye shall be able enough, as well as other kings, and then you may give your men somewhat. Your uncle is old, and I trust he will not live long. Ye are but a very beggarly king now. Ye have not to play [money to gamble with], or to give your servants. You are too bashful in your own matters – why do you not speak to bear rule, as other kings do?' The king replied, 'I am well enough, I need not.' Seymour continued, 'I will give Fowler money for you. If anything is said against me, do not believe it until I speak to you myself.'

Subsequently, the king sent notes on crumpled paper requesting money from the admiral, who was only too happy to oblige, thinking he was getting a greater hold on the king. The king must have felt that he was unable to trust his Seymour uncles, for he referred to Lord Parr, Katharine's brother, as 'mine *honest* uncle.'

Katharine fed her husband's hatred for his brother and the duchess. The Protector had behaved in a high-handed way with Katharine's property of Fausterne, and she complained in a letter to Thomas:

My Lord,

This shall be to advertise to you that my lord, your bro ther hath this afternoon made me a little warm. It was fortunate we were so much distant; for I suppose else I should have bitten him. What cause have they to fear having such a wife? Tomorrow, or else upon Saturday, at three o'clock in the afternoon I shall see the king, when I intend to utter my choler to my lord, your brother, if you shall not give me advice to the contrary; for I would be loth to do anything to hinder your matter: I will declare to you how my lord hath used me concerning Fausterne; and after I shall most humbly desire you to direct my answer to him in that behalf. It liked him today to send my chancellor to me, willing him to declare to me that he had bought Mr Long's lease, and that he doubted not but I would let him enjoy the same to his commodity, wherein I should do to his succession no small plaeasure, nothing considering his honour, which this matter toucheth not a little, for so much as I at sundry times

58

declared unto him that the only cause of my repair into those parts was for the commodity of the park, which else I would not have done. He notwithstanding, hath so used the matter, with giving Mr Long such courage, that he refuseth to receive such cattle as are brought here for the provision of my house; and so in the meantime I am forced to commit them to farmers. My Lord, I beseach you send me word with speed how I shall order myself with my new brother.

Princess Elizabeth and Lady Jane Gray had joined the queen at Chelsea prior to her marriage with Seymour. It seems there was some impropriety at some time after the admiral had taken up residence there. He would come barefooted and in his dressing-gown into the princess's bedchamber. Her governess,Mistress Ashley, described the scene:

At Chelsea, after my lord Thomas Seymour was married to the queen, he would come many mornings into the said Lady Elizabeth's chamber before she were ready, and sometimes before she did rise, and if she were up, he would bid her 'Good morrow', and ask how she did, and strike her on the back or buttocks familiary, and so go forth to his chamber, and sometimes go through to her maidens and play with them. And if the princess were in bed, he would put open the curtains and bid her 'Good morrow', and she would go further into the bed. And one morning he tried to kiss the princess in her bed, and this deponent was there, and bade him go away for shame.

Princess Elizabeth was now in her fifteenth year, and when Katharine found out what was going on she was displeased with both her husband and the princess, and sharply reproved the governess for neglecting to prevent such behaviour. If, horrible thought, the young princess had become pregnant through Seymour's reckless conduct, it would have brought terrible consequences on the head of Katharine as the royal guardian of Elizabeth. Thomas was an attractive looking man, and young girls found him irresistable.

It was soon discovered that the queen was pregnant.

Later, her husband would be harangued for 'marrying the queen so soon after the late king's death, that, if she had conceived straight after, it would have been accounted a great doubt whether the child born should have been accounted the late king's or yours, whereby a marvellous danger might have ensued to the quiet of the realm.'

Katharine, of course, was in raptures at the anticipation of a blessing which had been denied her in her three previous marriages. Thomas too was delighted, their feelings of paternity ammounted to a passion. Thomas escorted her to his principal baronial residence, Sudely Castle, Winchcombe, which he had specially fitted out as a sumptious residence for his bride. The queen had a princely retinue in attendance upon her at Sudely, included among her twelve ladies-in-waiting was Thomas Seymours niece, Lady Jane Gray and Lady Tyrwhitt. In addition there were eleven ladies of the house-hold extraordinary, as well as pages, grooms, porters and domestic servants.

Miles Coverdale, one of the leading lights of the Reformation, was appointed as the queen's almoner. He and several other ecclesiastic luminaries attended the divine worship ceremonies which Katharine caused to be performed twice a day, or oftener, notwithstanding the distaste of the admiral, who not only refused to attend these devotional services himself, but proved a great hindrance to all the pious rules his royal consort strove to establish.

Meantime tongues wagged and the admiral continually thwarted in his aspirations, raged like a bull. He talked openly of putting an end to the Protectorate to the Earl of Rutland.He mistakenly thought that he may get Wriothsley on his side, imagining that that worthy bore a grudge at the loss of his chancellorship, promising him that it would be restored. Wriothsley warned him, 'For God's sake, my lord, take heed what you do; I

60

hear abroad that you make a party. Beware how you attempt any violence. It were better that you had never been born, yea, that you had been burned quick alive, than that you should attempt it.' Lord Clinton warned him that if he kept on causing trouble he would lose the favour of his brother, the Protector, 'utterly and undo yourself.' Seymour shouted, 'I would you should know, by God's precious soul! I may lie better without him than he without me! And whosoever shall go about to speak evil of the queen, I will take my fist – from the first ears to the last!' Dorset intervened:'My lord, these words need not, for I think there is no noble-man that would speak evil of her, for he should then speak evil of the king that dead is. You have no cause to doubt therein, and I trust all shall be well and you and the Protector friends again.'

The Protector certainly seems to have suffered his brother's machinations with great tolerance, for he must have heard many complaints about him. His duchess advised, 'I tell you that if your brother does not die, he will be your death.'

On August 30th,1548, Katharine gave birth to a daughter. If Thomas was disappointed that it was not a boy, he did not show it, but wrote an eloquent desrcip-tion of the beauty of the new born offspring to his brother the Protector. Katharine was attended by her faithful friend Lady Tyrwhitt. Unfortunately she was stricken with puerperal fever. Lady Tyrwhitt described her sympstons: 'The patient is immediately seized with the strongest apprehention of her danger, and labours under vast anxiety, her countenance shewing indubitable marks of great suffering both of body and mind.' Two days before her death it was noticed that she did not mention the child and this was taken as a sure sign that she was near to death. On September 5th, Katharine made her will:

That she, then lying on her death-bed, sick of body, but of good mind, and perfect memory and discretion,and perceiving the extremity of death to approach her, leaves all to her husband. Witnessed by Robert Huych,M.D. and John Parkhurst.

In her confession, Katharine states that during her youth she held 'wrong opinions', which has been taken to mean that, like Sir Thomas More, she believed at that time that Humanism belonged within the established Church, whose fundamental beliefs and rights could not be changed. She confessed she was proud of her righteousness and of the fact that she was 'none adulterer, nor fornicator, and so forth.' She admitted that she loved wealth and luxury, and that she coveted to rule over men.

There were those who said her husband had treated her brutally and neglected her. That 'he had holpen her to her end.' There was also the usual rumour of poisoning, but Lady Tyrwhitt's testimony states that the admiral's manner towards her, when she was evidently suffering under the grievous irritability of mind and body incidental to puerperal fever, to have been soothing and affectionate.

Katharine Parr died at Sudely Castle on September 7th,1548, and was interred in the castle chapel. Her friend Miles Coverdale preached the sermon and Lady Jane Gray was among the mourners.

So ended the life of one of the most remarkable queens that this country has known.

A PRAYER OF KATHARINE PARR

HOW OFTEN HAVE I BEEN disappointed where I thought I should have found friendship: and how often have I found it where I least thought.

Therefore it is a vain thing to trust in man, for the trust and health of man is only in Thee.

Blessed be Thou,Lord, therefore in all things that happeneth to us: for we be weak and unstable,soon deceived & soon changed from one thing to another.

POSTSCRIPT

KATHARINE PARR'S daughter by Thomas, Lord Sudely, was named Mary. According to Agnes Strickland, she ought to have been the heiress of great wealth,and even if the act of attainder which had been passed on her father operated to deprive her of the broad lands of Sudely and the rest of his possessions, she was fully entitled to inherit the large fortune of the queen dowager, her mother, if only she had friends to assert her rights. She remained a little while at her uncle Edward's house at Sion; and then according to her father's dying request, was conveyed to Grimthorp in Lincolnshire, where the dowager Duchess of Suffolk (the former Katharine Willoughby) lived. There she was brought with her governess, Mrs Aglionby, her nurse, two maids and other servants. It has been stated that Mary died in her thirteenth year, but Agnes Strickland avers that she lived to be a wife and mother, the Duchess of Suffolk marrying her to Sir Edward Bushel.

Thomas Seymour continued his reckless career and wanted to marry Princess Elizabeth and still conspired to overthrow the Protectorate. A bill of attainder was drawn up against him and brought before the Lords on January 25th,1549. He was found guilty of high treason and beheaded on Tower Hill, March 20th,1549.

His brother, Edward, Duke of Somerset, was accused of trying to murder the Council and take over the government of the country. He was executed for high treason on January 22nd,1552.

John, 4th Lord Latimer, Katharine Parr's stepson, married Lucy, daughter of the Earl of Worcester, who bore him four daughters: Katharine, who married the 8th Earl Percy of Northumberland; Dorothy, married Sir Thomas Cecil, later Earl of Exeter; Lucy, married Sir William Cornwallis; and Elizabeth, who married Sir John Danvers. John Neville died in 1577 and there is a striking monument with his effigy in the church of

63

St.Michael the Archangel, at Well, near Bedale. The monument was erected at the expense of his son-in-law, Sir Thomas Cecil, in 1596.

The lordship of Danby Castle passed through marriage to the Danvers family, one of whom, Sir Henry, sold it off in parcels. John Dawnay bought the castle manor and was created Viscount Downe. It remains the property of the present Lord Downe and an annual Court Leet – the old medieval baronial court – is still held there.

An unpublished history of the Neville family by Agnes Strickland states that the 3rd Lord Latimer [Katharine Parr's husband] was buried in *Old St.Paul's*, which was destroyed in the Great Fire of London. However, the guide book to the church of *St.Michael the Archangel*, at Well, states that his body is in the Neville family vault, which the reader will recall, was his wish.

In the *Holy Trinity Church* at Kendal is the Parr Chapel, which was built by the Parrs in the early 14th century. Above each window is carved a maiden head, being the emblem given to Queen Katharine by Henry VIII. It is thought likely that the chapel was embelished by Sir William Parr, Katharine's brother, about 1545.

The chapel at Sudely was desecrated and unroofed by Roundhead soldiers in the English Civil War.Katharine's tomb and effigy were destroyed, but her body was discovered in its leaden envelope by some ladies in May,1782, and was said to be in perfect condition.

Sudely was bought by the Dent family, one of whom, John Coucher Dent, restored the chapel and Queen Katharine's monument in a most beautiful style.

LOCAL & REGIONAL HISTORIES BY KEITH SNOWDEN

KINGS IN RYEDALE
Covers 2,000 years of Ryedales association with royalty.
A delightful volume of which he can be justifiably proud.
Nicholas Rhea, ·*Darlington & Stockton Times.*
AUTHOR'S FIRST EDITION. £1.95. Post 33p.

PICKERING THROUGH THE AGES, *The Second Edition.*
Now revised and enlarged, with extended text and
many more pictures. Tells the story of the town from its
foundation in pre-historic times to the present day.
£2.70. Post 44p. ISBN 0 9527548 2 7.

HELMSLEY & KIRKBY THROUGH THE AGES
Here is the story of these two ancient Yorkshire market
towns and the many famous people connected with
them.
£2.85. Post 44p. ISBN 0 9514657 4 0

MALTON & NORTON THROUGH THE AGES
The story of these ancient sister towns, their noble
owners and famous sons.
REVISED EDITION. £2.85. Post 44p. ISBN 0 9514657 3 2

THORNTON DALE THROUGH THE AGES
Here is the story of one of Yorkshires prettiest villages and
the famous people connected with it.
NEW EDITION £2.95. Post 44p. ISBN 0 9527548 6 X.

SCARBOROUGH THROUGH THE AGES
The story of the Queen of English Watering Places.
REVISED & ENLARGED EDITION.
£2.95. Post 44p. ISBN 0 9514657 9 1.

THE CIVIL WAR IN YORKSHIRE
An account of the battles and sieges and Yorkshires
involvement. One of our best-sellers.
£2.95. Post 44p. ISBN 0 9514657 6 7.

WHITBY THROUGH THE AGES.
Pages from the history of this ancient Yorkshire sea port.
AUTHOR'S EDITION. £2.95. Post 44p.
ISBN 0 9527548 5 1.

KATHARINE PARR OUR NORTHERN QUEEN
The life and Northern associations of the last wife of King Henry VIII. A unique biography.
£2.95. Post 44p. ISBN 0 9514657 7 5.

MOORLAND MEMORIES
True tales from the Whitby and Pickering Moors.
AUTHOR'S EDITION. £2.85. Post 44p.
ISBN 0 9514657 8 3.

GREAT BATTLES IN YORKSHIRE
Recounting the many battles on Yorkshire soil from the Romans to the Roundheads.
NOW REPRINTED. £2.95. Post 44p.
ISBN 0 9527548 0 0.

A BOYHOOD PICKERING
Keith Snowden recalls living in the Twenties and Thirties, his school activities and life in wartime Pickering. This is social history in a autobiographical style.
£2.85. Post 44p. ISBN 0 9527548 2 7.

THE HOUSE OF YORK AT WAR
A Yorkist account of the Wars of the Roses.
AUTHOR'S EDITION. £2.95. Post 44p.
ISBN 0 9527548 3 5

THE ADVENTUROUS CAPTAIN COOK
The life and voyages of James Cook, R.N.,F.R.S.
Here is the life of this great Yorkshire-born navigator and his exciting voyages of discovery.
£2.99. Post 44p. ISBN 0 9527548 4 3.

KING ARTHUR IN THE NORTH
A study of this renowned historic figure.
AUTHOR'S EDITION £2.85. Post 33p.
ISBN 0 9527548 7 8.

ON SALE IN LOCAL BOOKSHOPS, OR DIRECT FROM THE PUBLISHER : CASTLEDEN PUBLICATIONS,
11 Castlegate, Pickering, North Yorkshire, YO18 7AX.
Telephone 01751 476227.
Post free on five or more copies.